Except for Love

New England Poets Inspired by Donald Hall

Except for Love

New England Poets Inspired by Donald Hall

selected & edited by
Cynthia Brackett-Vincent

Encircle Publications, LLC
Farmington, Maine USA

Except for Love: New England Poets Inspired by Donald Hall Copyright ©2019 Encircle Publications

Paperback ISBN-13: 978-1-64599-000-0
e-Book ISBN-13: 978-1-64599-001-7
Kindle ISBN-13: 978-1-64599-002-4

All rights reserved. No part of this book may be reproduced in any form by any mechanical or electronic means including storage and retrieval systems without express written permission in writing from the publisher. Brief passages may be quoted in review. Rights to individual poems and essays remain with authors.

Editor: Cynthia Brackett-Vincent
Book and book cover design: Eddie Vincent/ENC Graphics Services
Cover Images: Mount Kearsage—Alamy.com; Donald Hall—Steven Ratiner

Printing: Walch Publishing, Portland, Maine

Mail Orders, Author Inquiries:
Encircle Publications
PO Box 187
Farmington, ME USA 04938
207-778-0467

Online orders:
encirclepub.com

ACKNOWLEDGEMENTS

From the editor, gratitude to:

Doug Holder for his insightful reading;

Houghton Mifflin Harcourt for permission to use the quote, "There's no reason to live here except for love," which originally appeared in *Eagle Pond* by Donald Hall, 2007, Mariner Books;

Wesley McNair for his introductory tribute, "The Possibilty of Art: Fondly Recalling Donald Hall" which originally appeared in *The Boston Globe* on June 25, 2018 as "Donald Hall: a life of love, poetry — and the Red Sox";

Steven Ratiner for his 1997 photo of Donald Hall which graces the cover;

Eddie Vincent, husband and computer/graphic design guru, for constant support and for his gorgeous cover design.

CONTENTS

CYNTHIA BRACKETT-VINCENT
Preface — *Except for Love* — XI

WESLEY MCNAIR
Introductory Tribute — *The Possiblity of Art: Fondly Recalling Donald Hall* — XV

SHERRY BARKER ABALDO
Romance — 1
Lunatics — 2

MARY ANKER
Seapoint Beach — 3

L.R. BERGER
First Acts — 5
Duet — 6
Picking Raspberries — 9

EDWARD BRUCE BYNUM
What My Mother Told Me — 11

DAVID CAPPELLA
Like Snow — 15

JENNY DOUGHTY
I love you like an apple — 17
In the lean time — 18
As for the rose — 19

MAX ROLAND EKSTROM
At Mad River Barn — 21

MATT FORREST ESENWINE
Stone-Kicking — 23

ELIZABETH BRULE' FARRELL
Adirondack Chairs — 25

MONICA FLEGG
Checking for Ripeness At the Stop & Shop — 27

James Fowler
A Maple Family Reads a Syrup Poem — 29

David Giannini
After Years of Living — 31
Starting in the House — 32
Surprise Snow Squall — 33

Patricia Gomes
The Ocean Flows through Cracks Opened by Memory — 35

Kathleen McKinley Harris
Valentine's Night — 37

Scott T. Hutchison
Wild Honey — 39

Elizabeth Knies
These Days I Wake — 41
This Sailing — 42

Tricia Knoll
Obsessed Haiku — 43
Over Breakfast — 45

Katherine Leigh
Reverence — 47

Jim Mello
Tuba Skinny — 49

Mark Melnicove
The forsythia by the road — 51

Andrew Periale
Whisper — 53

Dawn Potter
Chores — 55
Ancient History — 56
Ghost Story — 58

Kyle Potvin
Waiting for the Results — 61

Jessica Purdy
Reflection   63

Gary Rainford
Striking Gold   65

Steven Ratiner
Autumn Leaves   67
Visiting Don   68
All the Time in the World   69

Dave Conlin Read
Afterparty   71

Russell Rowland
On the Death of Donald Hall   73
Dandelions   74
Mt. Kearsarge   75

Clemens Schoenebeck
Fixing what needs no fixing   77

John Surowiecki
The Other Side of the Sleeping Giant   79

Wally Swist
A Wild Beauty   81

Jeri Theriault
Make-Do Woman   83

Irene Willis
Ghost   85
The Milking   86

Warren Woessner
Farm House   87
March Clean-Up   88
Before Ice Over   89

Jane Yolen
Tending   91
No White Apples   92
A Ceremony of Losses   93

Contributor Notes 95

About Cynthia Brackett-Vincent & Wesley McNair 105

PREFACE

Except for Love

Cynthia Brackett-Vincent

This anthology aims to serve as a testament to the love we New England poets have for Donald Hall. It reminds us that he inspired us with his love — love of the written word, love of baseball, love for yesteryear in New England, love for Jane Kenyon, love for his day-to-day routine in New Hampshire reminiscent of Longfellow's words in "A Psalm of Life,"

Let us, then, be up and doing,
   With a heart for any fate;
Still achieving, still pursuing,
   Learn to labor and to wait.

Longfellow's words are near to my consciousness every time I re-read Hall's memoir, *Life Work*.
   I was introduced to Hall's work in 2005 in Wesley McNair's advanced poetry class at the University of Maine at Farmington. Throughout the semester, Wes handed out several packets of poems for his students to read, each labeled with what he was trying to teach us about poetry at that particular time. I remember "Sonnets," "Poems that Beget Poems," and "The Essential Image." It was in this latter group of poems that I found and fell in love with Hall's "Names of Horses." *O Riley*, I think, every time I re-read the poem or recall it. These are images that stay with you forever. I was in love. True to the title of Wes' second aforementioned packet, poems do beget poems. "Names of Horses" begot my 2019 "Putting Medusa Down":

Always the acrobat, leaping from bed
to desk, from bed to top of bookcase
as the cheetah leaps for the gazelle.
Always the queen, jealous enough
of my love to swat
a granddaughter
who vied for my attention.

Now she's lost two-thirds
of her body weight. She can no longer
clean herself. She cannot even climb

onto my lap. We have tried everything—
fluids, wet food to fatten her up.
Here we are after all efforts fail.
I lay her on her favorite fluff-blanket.

The vet walks in with the needle.
She looks up at me one last time.
The moment the needle enters
she is gone. I wanted to say good-bye
one last time. We will bury her ashes
in the old stone wall. I will receive
a mold of her paw-print.

In that moment I think of all
the cats gone by: O Poseidon,
Fluffy, Muffy, Smokey, Dusty,
O my Always-Queen Medusa.

I daresay his *life work* begot every poem in this anthology.

I had the pleasure of meeting Hall ten years ago in 2009 when he gave a reading at the University of Maine at Augusta for his then-new *Unpacking the Boxes: A Memoir of a Life in Poetry*. Then, seventy-nine, Hall noticeably sat as he read, and later inscribed books. I remember shaking his large, wrinkled hand. He must have wanted to move on to the next book-buyer as I gushed about how much *Eagle Pond* changed my life. I told him how much his sentence, "There's no reason to live here except for love," meant to me since moving to Maine seven years prior. After all, there's no reason to live in Maine and to have to shovel your roof—except for love. There's no reason to live in Maine and to have to put up with mud season—except for love. And there's no reason to live in Maine and deal with blackflies—except for love. If he did want to get rid of me, you'd never have known it, as he patiently listened to me with his good right ear, and as he inscribed, "for Cynthia with pleasure, Donald Hall."

Hall wondered about his legacy. With the gigantic body of work he left us—over fifty books including poetry, memoir, criticism, children's books, and essays, along with countless generous interviews—he needn't have wondered. He will inspire us for centuries. He inspired the hundreds of poets who submitted to this anthology. The poetic words of the thirty-five included here are now a small part of his legacy. We, his admirers, have wondered about the legacy of his beloved Eagle Pond Farm. I am thrilled that as of this writing, the homestead has been purchased by a couple that plans to preserve it.

Deep gratitude goes to *all* who submitted to this project—a testament to Hall's influence and inspiration. I think I have chosen the best of the best here. Can inspiration beget inspiration? Yes! May these poems move even more writers to become *inspired by their* favorite poets. I have been deeply touched by the many stories of Hall's generosity toward so many other poets, stories of Hall's commitment to returning correspondence to any and all who wrote to him. May we be inspired to give back, to encourage.

And let us always remember: There's no reason to (insert your own phrase here) except for love.

POSTSCRIPT:

10% of sales from this anthology will go to the Leukemia & Lymphoma Society to honor of Hall's wife Jane Kenyon. I trust Don would be pleased with this arrangement.

INTRODUCTORY TRIBUTE

The Possibility of Art: Fondly Recalling Donald Hall

Wesley McNair

I met Donald Hall in his ancestral farmhouse in Wilmot, New Hampshire, over forty years ago, when I lived nearby in my own farmhouse. We were introduced by two of his neighbors, former high-school students of mine who knew I wrote poems and thought we should know each other. Don was forty-seven then, a well-connected poet with several books to his credit. I, on the other hand, was thirty-four, and had no books at all, and with a family of four children, I had little time even to be a poet. But I did have a manuscript of poems, and after my shared visit with him, during which I hardly spoke, I sheepishly drew it of my coat, put it on his kitchen table, and got out of there as fast as I could.

After I got home, I reviewed my poems trying to imagine Don's encounter with them, and each seemed less impressive than the one before. But it turned out Don was drawn to them. In a letter I received two days later he wrote, "I am dazzled by your poems." I carried that letter around with me for days. I may have even slept with it. And in the end, I lost it. But I never lost those six liberating words. They helped carry me through years of expanding my manuscript, failing to place it, and at last publishing it. Don's letter also led to a correspondence and a friendship that lasted until the end of his life.

His early letters were full of advice, and some of it was very funny. After he saw a self-adoring biographical note that I'd written for *Poetry* magazine, he wrote: "I think it is wise not to load on the fellowships and academic appointments in your bios. If I were you, I'd try something that is quite reticent, non-academic, and non 'successful,' like 'Wesley McNair lives in New Hampshire, where he raises goats with eyes in the middle of their foreheads.'"

But when he wrote about the poems I sent him, he was uniformly serious, and the detail of his comments showed me that completing a poem required relentless revision. Patience was no less important. "Hold the work back for a long time," he said, "because a poem has a way of changing on its own, before anybody else's words get into it." In another letter he said simply, "The writing is what matters." Not half-baked lines and images, not even the book publication I was hoping for, but true words that stood still and meant what they said. What mattered above all, I understood, was the possibility of art.

I gradually learned that Don was engaged in his own struggle with the possibility of art. Just a year earlier, he had given up a position at the University of Michigan to relocate at his grandparents' farmhouse with his new wife, the poet Jane Kenyon, and the move had inspired work that took him beyond anything he had written as a tenured professor. His new poems remembered the boyhood summers he spent among the sheep and horses and stone walls of his ancestral farm, during which he listened to his grandfather recite poetry while milking his cows, and each morning watched his grandmother gaze at the beauty of the nearby mountain through her kitchen window. Once a poet of short lines, Don turned to long lines that allowed him to embrace the details of the place he recalled and to celebrate the connection he felt with Jane as the two of them took up residence there.

I remember Don's excitement when *Kicking the Leaves* came out in 1978, and his pleasure as he toured New Hampshire and elsewhere to read from it. The book and his readings resulted in a five-year appointment in 1984 as New Hampshire's poet laureate. I commemorated that event by way of a sweatshirt bearing the words "New Hampshire Laureate of Poultry." But what did Art think of the new poems? Don did not know. Sitting in his favorite living room chair at the farmhouse, he said to me, "You'll never really know whether you're any good as a poet, and nobody living can tell you either." Then he crossed his fingers, and in a comic follow-up, crossed his arms and legs, turning his whole body into a pretzel.

Yet the long lines and deep engagement of *Kicking the Leaves* gave Don an ambition he had never known before as a poet. Two years after the collection came out he wrote, "You know, I have not written a satisfactory poem — virtually not one poem — since that book...But I am working on long and ambitious things, and maybe they will not only be publishable but Immortal. And after all, that is the only thing worth thinking about." The poems he meant finally appeared in what may be his most important collection of all, *The One Day*, which surveys and denounces the greed and corruption of contemporary life in a range of voices that mix autobiography, history, and prophesy. Published in 1988, the book is more relevant than ever today, predicting the selfishness and depravity of Donald Trump's America.

Not long after he wrote *The One Day*, Don attempted another broad view of American life titled *The Museum of Clear Ideas*, which introduces a speaker he calls Horace Horsecollar. A combination of the old Walt Disney character and a Yankee sage, Horsecollar comments on the anxieties and folly of his age with a cool and witty irony. The detachment of his vision, at odds with the confessional impulse of poems in the 1990s, brought something new and different to American verse.

But Don did not forget his old subject of the grandfather's farm, going back to it again and again. In *The One Day* the farmhouse becomes the counterforce for America's corruption, a spiritual place where he and Jane spend each day writing poems as they create a third thing: "work's paradise." In later books, though, the ravages of time catch up with Don's vision of Eden. *The Museum of Clear Ideas*, written after his brush with cancer and fears of its return, alternately praises "the long white/ house that holds love and work together" and, through the voice of Horsecollar, mocks that view of the farmhouse as narcissistic. When Don reaches his final book of poems, *The Back Chamber*, having suffered the indignities of old age and years of grief for Jane, who died of leukemia, he describes the farm as a place of "cowbarns gone awry" and broken chairs ready for auction.

In "Meatloaf," a poem published in his eighth decade, he returns to the farm one more time as an old man who instructs the dead collagist Kurt Schwitters about baseball, a longstanding interest in Don's life and work. The aging speaker intersperses his meandering conversation with talk about his past life at the farmhouse, W.H. Auden, and a weird recipe he has invented for meatloaf. Just when we suspect the old man might be losing it, we notice that his apparently random thoughts have a pattern, which is derived from baseball's nine innings—nine stanzas with nine lines, each in nine syllables. The ups and downs of his life have a pattern, too, though it's sometimes sideways, with links to, among other things, the uncertain fate of the Red Sox in earlier seasons and a tour of the art museums of Paris.

In the end we see Don has adjusted the old poetic materials of his New Hampshire place to create a unique and wonderful poem—a "meatloaf" that resembles a modernist collage in its disparate ingredients. In the process he offers an homage to Kurt Schwitters and a celebration of art at the same time.

At the end of his poem Don offers a glimpse of himself as he writes "Meatloaf," revising its lines by "counting nine syllables on fingers/ discolored by old age and felt pens." Rediscovering him there as I write this tribute, I think of his advice to me forty years ago about my own revisions, and of his unshakable, life-long dedication to the possibility of art. I will miss him.

There's no reason to live here except for love.

—Donald Hall

Sherry Barker Abaldo

Romance

Love
does not last long
without a shower

without a fine meal

without flowers

or dreams, or wine, or compliments,
or islands—

Without wherewithal

without a future clean as a
blank face

without stupid hope

without the past
erased.

Lunatics

I lie
in bed with you
halfway
between our hearth fire
and the fullest moon
we'll ever live
to see,
supposedly.

I keep running
out naked
onto the doorstep
checking the moon
every few hours.
I tell you how white
and how clear
and how pregnant everything is.

You check the woodstove.
You wait for me.
You don't need to see;
you believe my reports.
You gather me again
and again into your arms
like kindling,
our moonlit skin blue as India gods.

Mary Anker

Seapoint Beach

the last winter storm
split
our apple tree
in half

the wound
orange and raw
against her dark bark
points to the sky
hands in prayer
all through April rain

in early May
mud season
she blooms fully
undaunted
from her bed
next to the saltwater marsh

we layer up
pull on dirty boots
make our way
down the meadow
long grasses slightly frozen
we catch each other
holding on
to pay our respects
her blossoms
already fading pink to white

Jamie,
  It seems that you have already discovered the wisdom of place — that is, wherever you are is home. The longing we feel for those who are not with us actually strengthens the bond.
  much love,
    Mary aka Ms. Anker

L.R. Berger

First Acts

Filling the teapot at the tap,
turning on the burner—

praise be for the day's first acts
requiring no imagination,
no choices of consequence.

You can be half asleep
and already a success at life,

draw encouragement
mastering the rituals of morning—

parting the curtains, reuniting
with your eyeglasses.

The looming hurdles of the day
begin to loom possible,
the heavy head of the earth

will not today spin off
on its orbit without you.

The water boils and you know
what to do, your cold feet

anchored again
to the map of the world.

Duet

The crow comes to the bare branch
and stays put

just outside
the ten paned window.

Sleet comes too mid-April,
winter clutching time —

a tangle of stiff limbs
impersonating the lifeless.

The crow grasps what is brittle,
scored bark inside a sheath of ice.

The first lines of a stanza
frozen on the desk between us.

Nothing wants to be said.

The crow is indifferent
to all things melodious.

We can just go on
seeing each other

because the branches continue
to hold back their green wings.

It's subtle. The crow tilts
its head. I tilt mine.

We see what we see
through the perch

of the other's
seeing—a woman

affixed to her own branch
who appears to be living

inside the confinement
of only one pane.

Eyes set to eye,
I rise in slow motion

to cross the room
as if to demonstrate

I am also a creature
made for freedom.

The crow steps into air
then hoists both wings

as if only an afterthought,
threading a path I can't see

through the mayhem
of twigs and branches.

My one wild wing,
mind of its own,

begins shamelessly
waving—

to the crow who mattered
more,

leaving the poem
unfettered to find itself.

Picking Raspberries

This morning I went out to the garden with an empty white bowl
and walked back inside with an empty white bowl.

In between and without decorum, I ravaged the vines
of late July, plucked and shoveled
palmfuls of sweet fruit into my mouth.

Someone watching might have said
now there's a woman whose body has slept alone
in a wide bed for a very long time.

My four year old godchild, Ella,
carried the empty white bowl for us yesterday
to pick raspberries for the first time.

It was left to me to explain about thorns.

We picked a few together, but then she disappeared
into her no-nonsense face, small fingers
threading thickets with intent.

From now on, she decreed after an uncommon
interlude of silence, we are going to pick raspberries
every time she comes.

It was the end of the season.
It was left to me to explain about seasons.

What could I say to her unforgiving eyes?
With what conviction expound

on the virtues of going without sweetness
to a mouth full of sweetness?

Edward Bruce Bynum

What My Mother Told Me

    For Donald Hall

My mother told me that when it was thunder and lightning
While the sun was shining
The devil was beating his wife.
I have awakened from dreams remembering this.
I remember Prince Valiant in the comic strips making a similar
    confession
Before his heart was carved up
And passed around like communion wafers
Among his soldiers who later assaulted the fort,
Then made friends with all the prisoners.
I remember a song composed
By tree spirits, orphans of the wind,
Who saw their own reflection even in the worms
Burrowing tunnels into the soil of matter
So the holy and the eternally living
Could return to the earth.
I know this because
After the rain passes
There is a monastic silence,
Clouds grow heavy, snore like great bears as they go off in the
    distance.
There is a stupid rule
That we must forget our past lives,
See them only as seeds in a pomegranate,
Wait for the energy to turn back on;
That we cannot walk naked amidst the sexuality of angels.
Like the story of Judas and the bits of silver
This is mostly *un*true
Although there was a being of light

For whom the fish would swim in and out of radiance for.
There is no theology of the throat,
No way the most powerful telescopes
Can scan the future
Where the great impersonator
Is smoking a cigarette and fornicating behind the stars.
Little evidence indeed for this except footprints of the dead
Appearing in soap bubbles then bursting
As the air swallows them into oblivion.
The soul is a musical sung
Mostly by amateurs. There are lots of missing notes
And not everyone shows up on time.
When the show finally happens
People are polite
Like at a foreign wedding.
Then the audience leaves quickly for the railroad tracks
Where the great aria is sung
And you feel you have ignited enough children
In this life
For the ferrymen to recognize you
As another professional wading souls across the river,
Seeking a bounty,
Knowing your work from the inside
As only the strongest and those who have never surrendered
 understand.
An apocalyptic dog is leaning into the sunset.
A grain of rice is holding on to its identity.
There is a wine brought to the harbors from ships
On only the warmest of summer nights.
There is a kind of murder easily forgiven
Because it is exercised by the priests.
What I mean is
My mother taught me the moon is a great yellow fish
Lolling around in the watery night.
That it was in disguise,
That there is an alien intelligence
Waiting for us to awaken when the heads of flowers became

    beautiful enough
And we can see the light
Within our own bodies showing us the way.
The pharaoh Akhenaten was the last messenger.
When he left his body slowly,
Like air does a balloon,
And returned to Sirius
He reported that we were an anxious species, temporal in our habits,
Suspicious of death
And its luminous initiations,
Unable to trust even the light waves tunneling between the stars.
Death remains the real master of ceremonies,
The smooth joke of gold, immutable and transcendent,
In the apothecary. Look for it. Invite it
Wholesale into the afternoons,
Into seawater, into the appetite of days.
It has a name for you
Clearer than a birdcall,
More exact than a diamond,
More porous and medicinal than a sprig of mint stolen
From a giant's garden charged with guarding the secrets of alchemy,
The dolphin's stellar religion.
They fold dark matter within their skulls you know, travel,
Are without an alphabet,
Enter music as a personal mythology.
My mother told me on my knees that faith
Is vernacular and translucent,
That I did not have to go far
To see a revolution begun by a poem,
Or witness opaqueness amid the funereal dignity of limestone and
   quartz.
'O yes' she would say,
'I have cousins in the afterlife waiting for me.
And when I go down to the river
I can watch the mules and the centuries flow past me
On their way to Armageddon.' When she talked like this
I could dream myself into a crow,

All black and militarily important,
Set my compass for the feral longitudes of the moon,
Know I would be greeted by swans
And those early missionaries to the earth.
She told me to honor silence
As though I was walking through the kitchen of a dead man's house.
She confessed she only loved me after I was born,
That there were several before me,
All deceased,
Who bore the name I kept,
That I could hear them at night
Drifting among the trees
Like tiny silver spiders on some incalculable quest.
She told me when suicides are successful
They become mirrors
Only vampires can see.
She confided in me there was intelligence in the skin of an apple
Put there by god. She warned me
The fish were angry with evolution
Because all their dreams were confined to water,
Because the moon would remain a remote genius,
Because their blood would never know the rain.
One afternoon
When the birds were silly with exhaustion
And the sun about to do its phantom drop down thing
Sliding under the earth,
I heard her reading from *the book of nails and milk*.
It was the last chapter.
It was the last few notes written in the margins
By the poet of the snakes.
I leaned in.
There was a beautiful fire in someone's hair.

David Cappella

Like Snow

Moments like snow,
melt unnoticed

until no longer
there. Gone.

A measure dissolves
in the waiting—

for the doorbell's ring
to split the silence

or the spruce shadow
to spear an oak leaf,

while galaxies spiral
and spin—

Jenny Doughty

I love you like an apple

I love you like an apple
loves the braided sweetgrass
basket, sturdy-framed with brown
ash, made to gather apples,
to store and cherish them, contain
within its own vanilla
that wine-tannic scent
of ripe and perfect apples.

I love you the way the round
basket loves the apple
whose blush and green and curved cheek
enhances its gold zigzagged
with brown, the way sunlight
as it brightens and fades
uncovers new colours
reflecting from one to other.

I love you when we, like
the basket and apples,
sag comfortably into
each other, not minding
snags and creases, holes,
the fraying of handles,
even though both basket
and apple move towards decay.

In the lean time

Ice encases my bare crab-apple tree:
the last tiny sour fruits hang
like crimson Christmas baubles.

Birds gather in their season's truce
and in the early mist jostle and heave
among the branches like party-goers
who have been up all night but are still
ready to dance, dressed in
the russet-red of robin breasts,
sharp-suited blue jays in sapphire,
white and black, discreet brown of
chickadees and the dull yellow
of one stray winter goldfinch,

all scattering ice-shells and apples,
leaving their three-toed claw-tracks
on the snow below the feast.

At the sun's first rays blackbirds,
who have patiently attended
like the orchestra at a ball
before the conductor arrives,
start to tune their curved notes,
turning the sunlight into song.

As for the rose

As for the idea of the rose, I don't know
if what I turn away from is not

the sadness of those who came
too late to see it bloom

or the silence of those who covered
its crown with soil against the frost

but the limitations of a flower,
its single perspective, view of a bed.

I live in the valleys
of my years, remembering

walks on the high fells as the hawk
remembers the contours of its soaring

and the steep and swoop to the slight
movement of a mouse. Even memory

feasts on fragments. I don't need
the past's presence when I have

its rose window, the pattern of panes
each with its own part of the story,

its view of the whole scene. My life is not
a rose despite the tight bud unfolding

whorl of petals, gold stamens,
crimson hips, bloom and death and rebirth.

Max Roland Ekstrom

At Mad River Barn

    For C. and M.

Yesterday at the swimming pool—
dozed under and sprouting meadow,
vanished except for the heaved roof
and split counter of the cabana
and changing room boarded up—
I learned you had recently divorced.
You took your vows not far from where
we toasted your son's graduation
and ambling by a brook you noted
what changed and what remained;
my kids stopped to look
for salamanders as you stood within
a forest of ferns and I daydreamed
into the beers ingested at the lodge
whose aftertaste of barley mixed
with ferns' sepulchral odor
and their phallic gesture of folk magic.
Today I think of you as I hear our
artless robin sing then stop—
how selfishly hurt I am
my friends divorced
without my permission.
Before the party broke up
you tried the door to the cabana,
a last peek at transformations past,
and I wanted you to put a shoulder to it.
A spruce discharged a redwing
blackbird, his wound of color seeming
integral to the gift of flight.

Matt Forrest Esenwine

Stone-Kicking

I kick my dreams
like stones in the road, watching them bounce
happily ahead while I
dawdle behind.
Old Buxton Road, still
damp from yesterday's storm,
smells of pine and mud. Gravel softly
sticks to slow feet while sunlight tries
through thick poplars
to warm a meandering path.
I kick another stone, watching it
quickly skip, kissing ground in its
own wayward curve…
The joy, of course, comes not
from picking it up, carrying it,
keeping it…
but from watching where it goes,
how far it rolls,
and, when it veers
to the slick road's edge,
setting it aright
with my foot
and flicking it
back to the
center.

Elizabeth Brule' Farrell

Adirondack Chairs

He sees the two chairs as broken,
the rotting pine legs near collapse.

A part of the yard for decades,
they had their place beside the bushes.

Deciding to discard the chairs,
he carries them one by one to the truck,

then turns around and brings them
to his workshop instead.

The sound of a rhythmic hammer
fills the air instead of a radio song.

He knows how to repair what needs
to be fixed and comes to me when finished,

before twilight settles behind the house,
inviting me to sit a while once more.

Monica Flegg

Checking for Ripeness At the Stop & Shop

I. Netting on a cantaloupe should be thick,
   coarse, and well-defined.

   Is your shield sturdy,
   tough, and well-refined?

II. Tapping the exterior of a melon should
    produce a low, deep sound.

   When you're tapped do you answer with
   a honking huff, or a calm response?

III. The base skin of the cantaloupe should
     be gold, not green.

   Think shine, not shade.

IV. If the stem of the melon is still attached,
    it was picked prematurely.

   Have you abided in the vine developing
   maturity?

V. The blossom end should have a
   sweet aroma.

   Sure, we all say; we do too!

VI. The blossom end should yield a bit when pressed.

    Perhaps we should have ended on aromas, you say.

VII. The blossom end should yield a bit when pressed.

James Fowler

A Maple Family Reads a Syrup Poem

An elegy for Donald Hall

At a 4th of July party with the in-laws
I ask about Donald Hall.
The eldest read that he had died
but never heard of him before.

I hand them Hall's *Maple Syrup* poem.
A dozen people, in silence, read it,
then the truth of who they were
rises to the surface of the gathering.

The maple producer thinks that rubber seals
are stupid; it would spoil the syrup.
His wife tells him, it was a canning jar.
Husband reads the poem again,
admits he'd missed the reference,
mind stuck on plastic jugs and metal barrels.

The group talks about Hall's story,
how the ending makes it great.
Then the business of the maple company
snares control of the afternoon,
as the eldest lectures the youngest
on how he should spend his money
on the old Christian camp for sale
adjacent to the family farm.
One of the other sisters' husbands
tells them the land would make
a great 'prepper' retreat, a place
where they could hold survival training.

I try to hold onto the poem's images
but when one of them screams,
"You're not listening to me!"
I drop Hall's bottle of syrup
and the whole world becomes sticky.

David Giannini

After Years of Living

in this hill-town, no one
is ever lost, even victims
of dementia rock on
family porches and look

across fields to blades of wind
turbines, remembering
hefting bales after haystacks,
some needles finally found.

Starting in the House

After a drenching rain,
                        I step out
and hear the pond's usually mild waterfall
one-tenth of a mile away

rushing with the voice of an old woman
screaming as she carries
her childhood doll by its legs,
the fall of its long hair across the spillway.

In a lifetime,
               she yells,
we come only once
through such water with the water we are.

Surprise Snow Squall

The sudden white hair
of everyone walking
without hats—you had

almost forgotten that
preparation. For eighty
winters you have entered

a house laughing at
the top of your head
fresh with an old man

beginning to melt; now
the difference is not just
that you are old, ashen,

but in the fire to come,
your body vanishing
like the sky's white air.

Patricia Gomes

The Ocean Flows through Cracks Opened by Memory

The plastic bag
covers the top row of rocks
on the miniature seawall
constructed by the small hands
of creative kindergartners.
It drapes, folds into whispers
becoming the black mantillas
worn to Wednesday noon Mass
at St. Anthony's
by the *good* neighborhood Memeres.
I watch the bag
bow in deference to the slightest breeze,
ready to fly off in a blink,
just like those old mantillas.
The Memeres got off their stiff knees,
genuflected, and turned, murmuring Bon Jour
to the other Dependable Memeres,
who took the mantillas off delicately,
so as not to disrupt
the perm that must hold until Saturday.
They fold those dainty lace scarves
into snap-tight plastic envelopes,
then tuck them into their weekday pocketbooks,
already planning the supper they would prepare
as soon as they made it back down the hill,
or up the hill,
or across the avenue
to home.
There, they will remember
the feel of cold hard stone, the scent
of salted-air, the lapping of March waves
as *they* constructed seawalls

while planning their future kitchens
where they would prepare suppers
for their own
creative kindergarteners.
"Bon jour, Simone."
"Bon jour."

Kathleen McKinley Harris

Valentine's Night

Thigh-deep, new-fallen powder snow,
starry, frigid February sky—
you, loving me, find excuse to visit daily,
show up tonight in the moonlight with snowshoes,
to invite me to walk with you in the woods—

no need for flashlights with such a firmament.
The malamute, joyful in his element, trots along.
You and I crunch and creak over cold-packed snow
to where plowed-town-road passes thrown-up-road.
We strap on snowshoes, turn up the old road bed.

As white hares with snowshoe feet hop,
with ease we walk atop the flawless field of snow.
We forget we aren't the first man and woman
to explore Jane Ann Hill until we lumber
past cellar holes, mere scrapes pathetic in their scale,

where other men and women loved, lived.
The last couple tried to make a go of it in the 1950s.
Under tonight's bright sky, the snow blanket
sinks over house and barn cellar holes just as soil
sags over body sites in neglected graveyards.

The half-grown pup plows snow furrows, wallows ahead,
takes side trips, his tongue lolling, mouth grinning.
With miles more on his legs than we log on ours,
he flounders, lags behind in our compacted tracks
until my snowshoes feel a ridiculous heft. I complain.

You point and laugh. The dog, his feathery forepaws
resting on my snowshoes, is hitching a ride. At hill crest

we turn into a copse of dark spruces, limbs heavy-laden
bent down top to bottom: by snow load about lopped off.
Dark and bone-deep cold close in. We head for the home fire.

Scott T. Hutchison

Wild Honey

>After Donald Hall's "Self-Portrait as a Bear"

Tilt the head back, sniff the air—clover
and apple blossom dapple the breeze,
a mellifluous incantation
moaning somewhere close, just out of sight,
hidden within a hollow. Drones beeline
straight back to home, mindlessly eager
to prove themselves to colony and queen.
Follow them. Love waits
at the end of that line.

Wild honey. You're always clawing your way
to it. A persistent thirst for nectar, fluid heartbeat,
feral swarming. Whatever impediments
forest themselves, attempting to impede your way—
they all weaken against instinctual pull: you
shoulder, brush, climb, fight off
whatever angrily wishes to sting you back—
but the pricks and poisons cannot prevent
your wreak of havoc, a luscious tearing apart.

Nothing out there presents, not nearly as sweet, as painful.
A taste of relentless truth. Nothing else provides
this momentary and boundless devouring
of star-filled night, cool creek water flowing,
earth flowering and worship; you escape into the honey
knowing: you too have been scented, you know by heart
that the hunt for you
is coming, flying straight through the trees.

Elizabeth Knies

These Days I Wake

alone, wondering where you are.
Light begins to spread
over the winter grass.
A bird makes a little two-note whistle
and another bird joins in
with something that couldn't be called a song.
The whistle-bird stops,
and then the other also stops,
leaving just the sound
of cars going by in the early morning
to wherever it is that they go.

This Sailing

On mornings like this we woke smiling
in the simple happiness of being together in bed
with the windows open and birds singing around us
in their shield of green.

Now the bed seems a poor craft,
neither moored nor captained.
It seems to be drifting somewhere, though —
everything is, after all.

I should be grateful that I am borne nightly
in such a simple way. I just get in,
and off I go until the morning,
when the birds begin again,

and I am not surprised
to find I haven't gotten anywhere —
the back yard and the garden are still there,
and the feathery pines that we loved.

It is effortless, this sailing.
It doesn't require any skill at all.

Tricia Knoll

Obsessed Haiku

After Donald Hall's "Distressed Haiku"

in the lining
of the silver drawer
a dried-up mouse

rabbit's foot
and a loose bell
remnant ring

icicles grow longer
as these days do
incrementally

scrape off boot ice
too many footprints
of the lonely past

our matching pajamas
synced dreams
four wrinkled rags

only mirth
took no notice
first sun in a week

night winds
divide intricate branches
as good a method as any

to get it in writing
old stones' pity
and the loss of moss

Over Breakfast

What if creativity is more than a thrown pot,
water color seas, and ode to honesty, our memoirs,
a sculpture of the first woman twisted
from juniper and rusted wire?
More than wind chimes tuned to hanging
beads, old forks and bluejay feathers?
Or the tundra haiku on a snow-blind page?
Something as fragrant as a sweet grass basket?

Let's add how we greet each other.
Our moving morning's invocation replaces
have a good one, how are you this one?

A blessing. Promise-based, how I make yours real.
What are you adoring? What are you escaping?
Is this twirling-we-are-in stirring your heart
as work on wing? Share fresh air with me?

Did you hibernate last night? Is now when your nut
breaks open? Does your wild aster seed fall
on cracked silt? Your fruited branch bend
under pears? Do you need help on this,
possibly the last, but also the best day
for adding on the warped wood abacus?

We don't need grants for achievements, prizes,
  no saving this cottage for admirers to peer
    through lace curtains. No museum shows.
Maybe a murmur in green waters
  lapping ashore as one
    or going separately. If we must.

Author's Note: *I can only imagine how two talented poets talk to each other in the morning, two poets who love each other deeply despite challenges. This is what I imagine in poetic form.*

Katherine Leigh

Reverence

As he reads his hands
Flutter above his head
Like falcons in release.
He mourns her, yet rejoices
In memories of Jane.

In words, your suspended agony
As you travel through time.
Jane awaits, she who is so still,
Her poems withstand her death.

The passion of a grasp,
The prolonged acceptance,
Two beings so embound
Rise together so
You lifted as she rose.

The final transition
Too abrupt, immediate.
Your life together was
The Poem; hence now
Prose.

Tell us of the angles of sun
The old barn and the ditch
The weeds disassemble the old car
The way the words insist.

Her pitch of clarity,
You say you miss her ear,
Jane's message, guidance,
Youth, her gardener-self
Who planted you.

So this end of tales,
Magical co-creation forever.
The throaty vibration of
Your advanced years carries
Reverence of what has been,
Is always mingled.

At Eagle Pond Farm,
Come every spring
White daffodils…

Jim Mello

Tuba Skinny

(American Folk Festival, Bangor Maine 2018)

Rev. Jim
is correct—
this band has drunk deeply
from the New Orleans fountain
and the music, is indeed, intoxicating

and maybe better for the soul
than the average sermon

though the subject matter
lies on the flip side
of your traditional hymn

what a deal the devil cut:
able to bulls eye
the soul's core
with washboard percussion
a tuba, a clarinet
and pathos as deep as
the delta mud

how can the spoken word compete
with such infectious rhythms
almost as irresistible
as Calvin's fabled Grace?

cartoon soundtrack music
when I was a child
able on this afternoon

to take me away
from my perplexities
and cleanse my pores
of the accumulated dust
from a very human week

Mark Melnicove

The forsythia by the road

The forsythia by the road
that we transplanted from the northern
edge of our land 30 years ago
when we were young
and in love
(as we are now,
only older)
have cobbled a thicket
of branches, a hideout, a nesting
ground for red-winged
blackbirds, harbingers
of spring, who have fought
blue jays for fertility
and won.

Andrew Periale

Whisper

First Draft

Whisper something you would whisper
to no other: say I am your monster,
your lightning strike, your chief of staff.
Say you want me, but use that
Donald Duck voice that makes children giggle.
Make a sound like the sea
in the shell of my ear and hum
a chorus from "Farewell to Tarwathie"
and I will imagine the soft explosions
of humpbacks surfacing, cold
salt spray soaking our clothes
dark men poised, their great harpoons
held high awaiting their moment

Revision 1

> *"The beginning of the poem has all these disparate images but shifts to an extended whaling metaphor."*
> —Keara

Shut the windows against the salt air, love,
and whisper: say I am your sea monster,
the eye of your hurricane, your laughing gull:
Say you want me, but use that pirate voice—
the harrrrsh tones that make children giggle:
Make a sound like the sea in the shell of my ear
hum a chorus from "Farewell to Tarwathie";
I want to hear the soft explosions

of humpbacks surfacing; cold, salt spray
soaking our clothes; dark men poised,
their great harpoons held high, waiting.

Revision 2

> *"I like the darkness that's implied when you say 'I am your monster.'*
> *I think it would have been nice if you continued on that throughout*
> *the rest of the piece."*
> *—Alyviah*

The still air of the graveyard chills me.
Take my hand and whisper; say I am
your monster, your nightmare, your leper:
Say you want me, but use that low growl
that makes children pull the bedclothes
over their heads, then hum a few bars
from the "Funeral March of a Marionette"
and I will imagine seven dolls
strung up by their limbs from an ancient
twisted oak. Find me, love, in the forest
at midnight, run your fingers through my fur,
your scent burning in my flared nostrils.

Author's Note: *When I tell my high school writing students how Donald Hall might do more than a hundred revisions of a poem, they stare, uncomprehending. So we write a poem. They critique me. I revise.*

Dawn Potter

Chores

When the girls and their grandpap
Carried the slop pail down to the barn,
They discovered the hog was getting ready to die.
It lay on one side.
Its tail twitched.
Muck had crept into its snout.
It was like a rotten log in a swamp.

The hog's breathing was heavy and slow.
Their grandpap shook his head and said,
Oh pig.
Now the girls knew for sure it was a goner.
They climbed up onto the fence
To watch the hog die.
But dying can take a long time.

Ancient History

Baby forgets the rain.
        Forgets how the lamplight
                spilled onto his page of homework.

He forgets the scent of dust,
        that old wet dog in the chair,
                that radio spitting its crackle of news.

Forgets the shouting in the kitchen,
        the way her voice rose, the way
                her plate slapped down on the counter.

He forgets the slam of the window,
        the cigarette ash drifting,
                the way her eyes tracked him

when he dropped his pencil on the floor
        Forgets her skinny fingers,
                their filthy sharp nails,

her stare like a chain
        yanking him underwater.
                Forgets how bad she smelled.

All he recollects
        is how she crashed back and forth,
                charging from burner to sink to burner—

scald slice boil scald slice boil scald slice boil—
        her flailing arms bloody with tomatoes.
                And Baby still sees those seven hot jars,

mashed vegetable flesh straining against the glass:
        how they hissed
                as she yanked each from the canner

and flung them screaming,
    one after one after one,
        out the yawing front door.

Ghost Story

      Someone very young
is picking out notes on a brown and humid piano.
              —*plonk*, pause, *plonk*—
      Whenever he touches middle C,
the key sticks
        —pause—
then sounds
        —*plonk*—
      and someone much older
is picking over a dishpan of strawberries.
She is culling ripe from overripe.
Her hands are stained with berry blood
        —*plonk*, pause, *plonk*—
Their sweet drunken attar
clouds the sour dishcloth,
the funk of sweat, and in the attic
        someone of no age
is picking up the faint vibrations
of two threadbare quilts, a stopped
clock, a foxed mirror.
Each object withholds motion, then briefly
trembles
              —pause, pause, *plonk*—
     and someone very young
presses a forefinger gently, forlornly
onto middle C, forcing it into
sticky silence
              —*plonk*, pause—
     and outside the yawning window
a cardinal, red as berry blood, trembles
from birch to pause to birch,
      and in the attic
     —*plonk*, *plonk*—
a board creaks, the clock

groans, two browning quilts ripple in the dusty
draught, and downstairs
      someone much older
shivers
      at something like a mirror,
      some brief, faint song
      of no age

    —pause—
               —and pause—
                           —and pause—

She thrusts aside her dishpan
    —*plonk*—
         and drives the window down.

Kyle Potvin

Waiting for the Results

      After Donald Hall's "Her Long Illness"

I am Jane. I am Ellen. I am Julia. I am dying
more slowly than they, but cancer is
lurking. Smoke in the throat, blowing simple
rings: rising, rising, rising. There she
goes, then her. And her. I said
I would remember them but what's
to say I am saved? Worst
if the breast is
guilty again. Or the toe with its dirty cells. The
blood, bone, I am them. No separation.

Jessica Purdy

Reflection

After a photograph by Phyllis Meredith

That the girl wears boots in calf-high water
must mean spring, the water cold
or maybe the lake bed's rocky.
The trees' fairy tale green, broad
leaves lap their lush tongues
against the surface overspread
with gold reflecting sun.
I remember feeling as if my body
were my own.
The way she holds the dog tucked
under her arm like a future baby;
the way the birds must sing to her
I can't hear from where I am
stuck solid in winter.
Dawn here only seems spring-like
with its brief ovation of pink
to an overcast western sky.
She's as surprised to see me
as a deer might be,
standing inside these rings of mirrored green.

Gary Rainford

Striking Gold

I pass groceries to Bobbie
from the counter, and she shuttles
each item into the refrigerator:

cases of Boost on the bottom
shelf; mandarin oranges in juice
on the door; Kraft singles go

in the cheese bin; a dozen hard
boiled eggs are assembled on a plate,
then covered with plastic.

"Mom, I have a surprise for you,"
I tell her once she's done fussing, done
rearranging the Chobani.

Digging into my front pocket
I can't wait for Bobbie's red carpet,
Barbara Stanwyck smile.

"Cup your hands," I say and drop
her bracelet-watch into them. "I had
a jeweler replace the battery."

"That's not my watch," Bobbie
scoffs. "What did you do with my good
watch? All my things disappear!"

"Mom, that is your watch. Read
the inscription." Fitting the Timex
over her wrist she examines it

as if she's appraising the heavens
for truth and says, disgusted, unlucky,
and cheated, "I'll make do, I guess."

Steven Ratiner

Autumn Leaves

In the old haiku: a brocade
adorning the river—but later,
the mud-umber rags snared
on fallen branches, and next spring,
or the next, the rich black muck
along the bottom where hatchlings
tail into the current, nosing for morsels.
This morning—*my* morning:
fallen leaves, fallen poems,
the darting fish of words without
the mouths to sing them, the minds
to keep their course true, wading waist-
deep, sting of Kearsarge snow-melt,
the slime of old dreams between
bare toes, and every so often some-
thing bubbles up to the surface,
dim April syllables, I may
or may not even notice.

Visiting Don

In Memory of Donald Hall

In the dream, I'm back at Eagle Pond.
One window's filled with the heavy heads
of Jane's peonies—and the other, snow
banked up high against the darkened barn.
You were inscribing a book for me with
a silver pen. How sloppily the dead write.
The D was a shriveled moon mired above
an unmown field. And what homeless poet
could survive inside that lean-to of an H?
You were making a joke about how you
wisely packed an extra sweater—the ground-
freeze running eight feet deep this year,
my little boat moored at six!
Great brown islands on a parchment sea—
the liver spots across the back of your hand.
I shivered, watching as you penned *for Steven*
into the book of dried leaves and dead horses—
like mercury, those *vowels of bright desire*—
then, startled awake by my industrious neighbor,
mowing her lawn at seven a.m. By now,
you'd have been up for hours, wading into
manuscripts, and so I too should be.
Work itself must be the *prodigy* that keeps
any of us close, safe, whole.
Or is it ink? Or sleep? Or sorrow?

All the Time in the World

    For Don and Jane

One morning, amid the humdrum,
God erupts in the marrow of her bones.
His whisper snakes its way
down the colon's dark corridors.
Something knocks on the door of the medulla,
stops, leaves its mark.

Another morning, we find ourselves
cowering by the kitchen sink,
convulsed in tears, felled
by a broken fruit bowl,
a bit of burnt toast.
Please Lord, I've learned my lesson…
Our prayers take on the form
of bargain, appeasement —
If I never drink again,
if I learn to love,
if I if and if for the rest of my life…

We begin to make plans,
set our affairs in order,
inform the family,
spend long afternoons weeping with friends
or re-reading Whitman in the bath
or clawing on hands and knees
through the garden beds, prying apart
knots of iris and planting next year's allium.

One morning we taste salvation
in a swallow of milk.
There is frost scaling the bedroom window
and we take it for heaven.

Through your nightgown, I watch
the shadow of an arm
run a brush through your hair,
again, and slow again,
your small breast buoyant,
and suddenly I am another man.
Lying together, we whisper
in each other's ear: *all the time in the world,*
the way we used to say *I love, I love.*
Forever is another brevity and we
make peace with our portion.

Dave Conlin Read

Afterparty

We don't bid our dead Godspeed to the afterlife
the way we did, in churches, where weeping echoes
off walls or gets absorbed by pipe organ blasts,
while incense spirals from an acolyte's censer,
and the minister intones his woeful sound.

After we lowered our dearly departed into the ground,
back at the church hall there would be baked ham,
casseroles, and pies, supplied by neighbors and aunts.

Today, in function rooms, where event planners
have laid out aromatherapy diffusers and flowers,
we get right on with the afterparty and mingle,
nibbling fruit, veggies, and tiramisu, while a playlist,
synced to a slideshow, loops in the background.

Russell Rowland

On the Death of Donald Hall

Once he ceased vaulting the rainbow
of verse to rest in the essay easy chair,
I thought that epitaph enough. It is
our way to want more of our betters:
Big Papi must homer again, Schubert
finish that Unfinished Symphony.

He joins old ghosts in the old house
on the old farmstead at Eagle Pond.
It is a family reunion which excludes
the living: their words yet un-shelved,
acknowledgement of death equivocal,
agnostic to its unassertive orthodoxy.

So many deaths. Broken draft horse
tipped into a hole to fertilize clover.
Estranged friend gone, unforgiving
and unforgiven. The potency to rise
to sexual occasions. Jane, who was
supposed to live to bury her Perkins.

Where, autumn leaves of yesteryear?
The jack-o'-lantern in the cemetery
no longer laughs or cries; his candle
sinks into its wax. He gave us more
deaths than we wanted—yet in this,
his last, we consent to own them all.

Dandelions

As far as the eye can see —
a buttery Milky Way overspreads
acres of May's green firmament:
weeds by profusion transfigured
to a new Eden, equally transient.

The very same eye narrowed
at the Samaritans, at the poor
we always have with us — a squint
that let in neither color nor beauty;
that delayed no errand at the sight.

The mowers perhaps are waiting
to throw their rotary blades
into noisy high gear, and leave
a harvest of severed yellow heads
for vintners, for brewers of tea.

Spared the grim reaper's scythes,
those button-blondes will whiten
like other once-young brevities,
until breezes sweep them away
from stem and root and memory.

The eye itself starts to go opaque:
no yellow, little hope, less light,
until the surgery. Healed, it waits
for withering winds to moderate,
sells all it has, and buys the field.

Mt. Kearsarge

>After Donald Hall's "Mount Kearsarge"

We lifted our eyes to Hall's blue ghost:
the old poet, all whiskers, on his porch;
a widow, in the house she needs to sell;
I from the Ossipees' opposite sentinel.

Whence cometh our help? Help comes
from the Lord: He who made Kearsarge
and Ossipee made whiskers, and widow,
and me. In the little church in Danbury,

where gather two or three, and incense
rises from the coffee pot and casserole,
and every minister stays a year or so,
this is the only sure and certain hope.

Where was one grave we now see two.
Well, what of it? Death need not part.
From the farmhouse groaning with age
an elderly man of many meters is gone;

but now comes a woman rustic strong,
with some of the same rhythms in her.
Pages turn in the wind without fingers.
You bury the body but never the song.

On the summit, ancestral spirits gather,
older than poetry. We take them for
cirrus, lupine, white-throated sparrow.
He who died taught us our metaphors.

Clemens Schoenebeck

Fixing what needs no fixing

> *I tinker with little things,*
> *and it is my greatest pleasure in writing.*
> —Donald Hall

Like an exuberant gardener
he digs up and replants his poems,
as many as two or three hundred times
until they reach full bloom.

He nurtures and feeds, divides and weeds
what takes away from the truth of each line;
deadheads spent blossoms, restructures
a dark phrase into a patch of sunshine.

Nothing wilts on the page.

I remember how he signed my copy of *Without*,
his elegy for Jane, where, on page 80
he circled the phrase, *as we watched*, arrowed it
to the line above where it replaced the words
over the years, bringing it all into the present moment…

How does the poet make better what is already good?

John Surowiecki

The Other Side of the Sleeping Giant

       After Donald Hall's "The Sleeping Giant"

In Meriden, Silver City of the World
and home of Connie Mack and Big Ed Walsh,
my Uncle Steve (hall-of-fame boxer) and Uncle
Sarge (national duckpin champ),
we couldn't see the behemoth,
asleep or otherwise,
in our ancient blue hills.

What we could see was a locomotive,
sleek and futuristic, hissing and chugging
its way into our actual railroad station:
so as one train continued on
to New York City,
the other was bound for a more rarified place
where giants never died.

Wally Swist

A Wild Beauty

> *Every poem is a momentary stay against the confusion of the world.*
> —Robert Frost

To salvage the last
of the heirloom roses
after the morning rain,
to place them in
a clear crystal vase
without water,
so that I may dry

the florets
and remaining petals,
to preserve
their sweet fragrance,
to nourish
ourselves against
heartache. The snipped

wild red roses
drying in their vase
are prayers imploring us
to look within
to find the flame
flickering with such
a wild beauty

that it extinguishes
the smothering darkness.
Salvaging the last roses

this morning in the rain,
my body awoke to
the coolness, to a scent
that exhilarates, which, if

we can preserve it,
nurtures us through what
are calculated avaricious
rants, vortices of disorder,
with what serves us
as an uncanny sustenance,
its own inexplicable elixir.

Jeri Theriault

Make-Do Woman

>For Mamie DuLac Drouin (1884-1963)
>After Donald Hall's "Ox-Cart Man"

In October she snugs her kitchen plot
with raked leaves and rough boughs, tells the sleeping roots
to rest, lays pine needles thick on the roses she trusts
to no one else and moves parsley to her sunny sill.
Winter clothes come out now,

for mending and hand-me-downs. Apples sugar
her kitchen, making jelly and sauce for the cellar shelf.
November evenings by the fire she knits with dyed wool
from Armand's up-the-road sheep, Bill snoring
over his paper. She makes

fudge for the first fair, fruit cake and meat pies
for after Midnight Mass. All of it keeps nice in the downstairs
chest freezer, even sweet-dough for cookie-swaps.
January she sews new curtains, underwear
and linens. Tats lace to sell

at Easter Bazaar. Plans her next garden. Raised
beds. More roses. All spring and summer that digging
and weeding. Not truly needed with Pa's good store
nearby, but it fills her up, this bounty from her own
hands, like the bounty

of seven children—eight if she counts Abraham,
who died. June 23 she thinks how old that sorrow, and pastes
her cut-out recipes in a wide-ruled book near the made-up
stews in her shaky scrawl. August tomatoes
and pickles, the start again

of canning. Patching school clothes and sometimes
on a still afternoon, she wades the cool creek, her hot feet
splayed, as she listens to the children splash and shout,
listens to the crows and jays in the tall pines
listens to Bill's mower on the hill.

Irene Willis

Ghost

> *…the outline of absence defined*
> *a presence that disappeared…*
> —from Donald Hall's "Kill the Day"

When she comes to see me now
on a new leash

with her sad eyes

she walks on soft paws
through my new rooms

with the old chairs
and the memory

of her master
inside.

The ghost she's become
is their absence defined—

his ghost and hers—

the door closed forever
behind.

The Milking

Almost unbearably intimate
to be grasping the body parts
of a being as mammalian
as myself—allowing me to do
this to her, my fingers pulling
like this, the drops from her
body tinkling into the pail
and then, as I grow stronger,
streaming into it, she turning
her head slightly to face me.
She and I producing this—
satisfaction—together, not
taboo but approved of and
wholesome. All over the world
I think, men and women are
doing this to females in their
barns—to the great, surrendering
cows who yield themselves to
callused thumbs and fingers,
who let—no, even beg these
dominating creatures to do
this to them and who feel,
when the pail is full, *relieved*.

Warren Woessner

Farm House

The first night in the country
I woke in the dark dark—
put my hand in front of my face
and couldn't tell my hand
was there.

Got a night light the next day.
Just one Christmas tree bulb
but so bright in the bathroom
I had to close the door to sleep.

This year we're back
and it's burned out.
I turn off the bedroom lamp
afraid to admit I'm afraid
of the dark we paid so much for.

But light pours through the blinds.
It's from a half moon,
unbreakable mirror,
sending sunlight
to this half of the earth
for free.

March Clean-Up

Today the trees
have an early spring wind
in their hair,
combing out the tangles
with a stiff brush,
shushing the little ones—
making them bow down
then stand up straight,
and hold out fresh clean hands
for me to admire.

I find an elder long dead
but still standing.
Years of woodpecker
and insect holes
perforate frail cellulose bones.
I should let nature
take its course,
but being in that course,
I give it one good push,
watch it crash
from the air-making world
back to making earth.

Before Ice Over

    For Iris Freeman

At dusk, one by one,
hundreds of gulls fall
out of the leaden sky
onto the lake, already
beginning to close
its lid for winter.

We call them
by their names,
recognize bill color,
molt, age, species—
see everything
but living beings—

finding their spots
for the night, calling out
to kin, to neighbors.
Afloat on freezing waves,
they turn together
into the north wind.

While, on shore, wrapped
in down coats, hats and gloves,
we strain to see
every last one
in the failing light, like
it was some miracle.

Jane Yolen

Tending

There is a moment each day
when I sit on your bed,
carefully, for the creases hurt.
And if I clear my throat
you feel it in your bones.

But still you crave the nearness,
as if love runs like a wire
between us. Sometimes
you put your hand on my wrist
as I bring you a glass of water.

There is no visible spark,
but I can feel it and know
you are still alive
in that old body, as I am
in mine.

No White Apples

When my husband had been dead a week,
I turned over
and felt his left leg
beneath me
which was strange, because
I now slept
on his side of the bed

his bathrobe draped my shoulders,

 ginger and the taste of dirt

if he whispered
I would straddle him

kissing his long face,
               the pale skin
                    still tight with death

A Ceremony of Losses

> *Old age is a ceremony of losses.*
> —Donald Hall

The door yawns open, I step in.
A collection of chairs sings my praises.
The sofa harrumphs like an old uncle.
The schoolmarm desk makes a speech
about honor and hard work.
It's the only speech she knows.
A plastic tray serves a round of drinks,
though only mine has liquid in it.

I salute the photos on the wall.
The Losses look back at me,
smiles softened by the glass' glare,
the age of the paper
on which they're printed.
I remember most of their names,
though only recall their faces
as they exist in the pictures.

Yes, it's a ceremony, like all such,
full of contradictions:
elation hand-in-hand with sorrow,
and a smattering of regret,
all sharp-edged and bound in black.
We whisper about the old times,
make up the half we forget.
But at least I'm here to enjoy it.

CONTRIBUTOR NOTES

SHERRY BARKER ABALDO: "Donald Hall inspires my work through his poetic alchemy where erudition meets eros, his instinct of time and place, and our link, Wes McNair. The longer you look at Hall's lines, the more there is to see; he achieves the feeling of inviting the infinite." Abaldo grew up in Union, Maine, where she now lives. She majored in English Literature, magna cum laude, Phi Beta Kappa, honors in creative writing at Wellesley College. She researched and wrote scripts for award-winning TV documentary films (PBS, History Channel). Abaldo missed fiction, got accepted to the University of Southern California film school, MFA film production, and optioned feature film scripts. Always, she wrote poetry. She returned to Maine from LA, with boxes and drawers and scratch pads. On her second Dibner Poetry Fellowship, she went to Big Lake, Grand Lake Stream with Wes McNair who basically consolidated everything. Her poems have appeared in *the Aurorean, Northern New England Review, Rattle*, and more, including the new anthology of fifty Maine women poets, *Balancing Act 2*.

MARY ANKER: "Words fill my life: storyteller for siblings, a proud essayist, journalism, advertising, layout and design, English teacher, poet. Learning from Haystack and Breadloaf teachers. Being asked to perform. Sending my poems out on their own. Studied with Naomi Shihab Nye and Kim Stafford. Had five poems in *Piscataqua Poems, A Seacoast Anthology*; one earning third place. 'a small rotation' was analyzed in the *Portsmouth Spotlight*. Long ago at Jazzmouth, I asked Donald Hall some I'm-sure-insipid question; he gently put his face in mine and gruffly recommended, 'Write! Write! Write!'"

L.R. BERGER'S collection of poems, *The Unexpected Aviary*, received the Jane Kenyon Award for Outstanding Book of Poetry. She's been the grateful recipient of fellowships and support from the National Endowment for the Arts, the PEN New England Discovery Award, the New Hampshire State Council on the Arts, and The American Academy in Rome. With Kamal Boullatta, she assisted in the translation from the Arabic of, *Beginnings*, by Adonis (Pyramid Atlantic Press). She lives and writes in New Hampshire, where Donald Hall's day to day faithfulness to the fibers that, *braid the ordinary mystery*, is a perpetual inspiration.

EDWARD BRUCE BYNUM is a licensed clinical psychologist currently in private practice in Hadley, Massachusetts. He is the author of several books in psychology and poetry. Most recent books in psychology include *Dark Light Consciousness*, *The African Unconscious*, and *The Dreamlife of Families*. New books in poetry include *The First Bird*, *The Magdalene Poems: Love Letters of Jesus the Christ and Mary Magdalene*, *The Luminous Heretic*, and *Gospel of the Dark Orisha*. His volume, *Chronicles of the Pig & Other Delusions*, won the national Naomi Long Madgett poetry prize. See his author page on Amazon. Hall's influence: "I heard his voice on the radio and read his interviews in *Poets & Writers*. He was only a few years older than me. He lived in a contiguous state and he lived as though poetry was his blood. His verse was direct and honest and serene and beautiful and bold."

DAVID CAPPELLA, Professor Emeritus of English and 2017/2018 Poet-in-Residence at Central Connecticut State University, has co-authored two widely used poetry textbooks, *Teaching the Art of Poetry: The Moves*, and *A Surge of Language: Teaching Poetry Day to Day*. He won the Bright Hill Press Poetry Chapbook Competition in 2006. His manuscript, *Gobbo: A Solitaire's Opera*, will be published by Cervena Barva Press in 2019. His novel, *Kindling*, has been called "a powerful and devastating coming-of-age story." "Donald Hall's poetry showed me how to imbue my writing about experiences in and perceptions of the natural world with the metaphysical." Visit his university website: http://webcapp.ccsu.edu/?fsdMember=249

JENNY DOUGHTY is a former English teacher and Education Advisor to Penguin UK. Originally British, she has lived in Maine since 2002. Her poems have appeared in *the Aurorean*, *Four Way Review*, *Naugatuck River Review*, *Pulse online review*, and *Gathered*, an anthology of contemporary Quaker poetry. She serves as President of the Maine Poets Society. Her first book of poems, *Sending Bette Davis to the Plumber*, was published by Moon Pie Press in 2017. "Donald Hall's poems of love and loss, of place and displace, touch something deep in my own experience of these things."

MAX ROLAND EKSTROM writes: "My poetry has appeared or is forthcoming in publications including *the Aurorean*, *Comstock Review*, *Grasslimb*, *Hubbub*, *Mudfish*, *Poetry Quarterly*, *Rockhurst Review*, and various others. I am anthologized in *Hunger Enough: Living Spiritually in a Consumer Society*. I am also the proud recipient of the 2004 Emerson Graduate Award in Poetry from Emerson College, where I received my MFA." True to Hall, Ekstrom writes in both free and formal verse.

MATT FORREST ESENWINE writes: "I have had several poems published in various journals/anthologies including *The Licking River Review*, the Tall Grass Writers Guild's *Seasons of Change*, *Trigger Warning: Poetry Saved My Life*, and others. My poem, 'Apple-Stealing,' was nominated by the Young Adult Review Network for a Pushcart Prize, and I have a poem in *National Geographic's* new anthology *The Poetry of US*. Donald Hall has inspired me not only by his geographic proximity—I live near the base of Mt. Kearsarge—but also by his use of nature to help us understand the deepest and most difficult truths about ourselves."

ELIZABETH BRULE' FARRELL has published poems in *Beyond Forgetting* (Ed. Holly J. Hughes, Foreword by Tess Gallagher), *Earth's Daughters*, *The Healing Muse*, *Paterson Literary Review*, *Poetry East*, *Proposing on the Brooklyn Bridge* (Ed. Ginny Lowe Connors), *Spillway*, and others. She was the recipient of The Louise Bogan Memorial Award for poetry. She was born and bred in New England with a brief time spent writing advertising copy in Chicago before returning to the place she most loved. She admires Donald Hall's expression of his relationship with Jane which moves her to appreciate the daily life of her own marriage.

MONICA FLEGG lives on Nantucket Island where she walks dogs of various breeds, reads poetry of all creeds, and generally has a lot of fun. Her writing has been published in numerous journals including *Ruminate*, *Snapdragon*, and *Unbroken*. She's the author of the chapbook, *Somewhere in the Cycle*. "Donald Hall has inspired my writing by digging into everyday life with a reverence that transforms simplicity into sacredness."

JAMES FOWLER, retired Navy, lives in Charlestown, New Hampshire, and has had over 250 poems and over fifty short stories or flash fiction published in various journals and anthologies. He edited the poetry anthology *Heartbeat of New England* (Tiger Moon Publications, 2000) as his final practicum for his Master's in Environmental Science. Finishing Line Press published a chapbook of his Japanese forms, *Connections to This World*, in 2012. His book, *Falling Ashes*, was volume VII in Hobblebush Press's Granite State Poets series. He once attended a Donald Hall poetry reading at the Fells Historic Estate in Newbury, New Hampshire. He had to sit in the next room where he couldn't see Hall, but just hearing Hall's voice inspired him. Fowler was moved by the fact that so many people came to listen to Hall's voice. It made him believe he could be a poet.

DAVID GIANNINI'S collections of poetry include *In a Moment You May Be Strangely Blended*, *The Future Only Rattles When You Pick It up*, *Faces Somewhere Wild* (Dos Madres Press, 2017; 2018; 2019) and *Traveling Cluster* (New Feral Press, 2018). His work also appears in national and international literary magazines and anthologies. "I met Don Hall on April 17th, 1982 at his reading in Brattelboro, Vermont, where he was nearly in tears after reading his *in memoriam* poem to his recently dead friend, the poet James Wright. His poetry and prose of rural life continued to inspire."

PATRICIA GOMES, currently in her second term as Poet Laureate of New Bedford, Massachusetts, is the former editor of *Adagio Verse Quarterly*. She has been published in numerous literary journals and anthologies. A 2008 and 2018 Pushcart Prize nominee, Gomes is the author of four chapbooks. Her recent publications include *Muddy River Review*, *Star*Line*, *Tidings*, and *Underground Writers*. Ms. Gomes is the co-founder of the GNB Writers Block as well a member of the SciFi Poetry Association, New England Horror Writers, and Massachusetts Poetry Society. "The flow, the pace of Donald Hall's work never fails to quell life's chaos."

KATHLEEN MCKINLEY HARRIS, author of the chapbook, *Earth Striders* (Finishing Line Press, December 2017) is the winner of the Ralph Nading Hill, Jr. Literary Contest with her poem, "Bear Fear." She wrote the children's book, *The Wonderful Hay Tumble* (William Morrow, Jr.). "I feel close to Donald Hall because his love for New Hampshire is like my love for Vermont and because his poem, 'Names of Horses,' is kin to my Morgan horse poem, 'T.D.' He also dealt with the sickness and death of his wife as did I with the heart disease and death of my husband, Everett."

SCOTT T. HUTCHISON'S work has appeared in such publications as *The Georgia Review*, and *The Southern Review*. He served as the State Director for the New Hampshire Young Writers' Conference for thirteen years (working with the NH Writers' Project), and has served on the rotating faculty of the New England Young Writers' Conference (held at Bread Loaf each May). Hutchison is the author of two books of poetry, *Reining In* (Black Bird Press), and *Moonshine Narratives* (Main Street Rag Publishing). "Donald Hall is part of the New Hampshire landscape—I'm happy that, in the grand scheme of things, I can't even count the number of times I was privileged to see him read over the years, in venues both large and small. He was a generous spirit."

ELIZABETH KNIES is the author of five collections of poetry, including *The New Year & Other Poems*, *Streets After Rain*, *From the Window*, *White Peonies*, and *Going and Coming Back*. She holds master's degrees from the University of New Hampshire and Boston University and has published poetry, essays, and reviews in numerous publications. From 2007-2009, as the Poet Laureate of Portsmouth, New Hampshire, her current home, she created a multi-faceted project called "Surprised by Joy." She knew Donald Hall and Jane Kenyon over the course of many years and admired their work, especially Don's heartbreaking *Without*, published after Jane's death.

TRICIA KNOLL is an aging Vermont poet who hopes to be writing after the age of eighty. She loves rural life and is captivated by a love affair that endured and nurtured two creative souls. Her poetry collections include *Urban Wild*, *Ocean's Laughter*, *Broadfork Farm*, and *How I Learned To Be White* which received the Gold Prize for Poetry Book Category for Motivational Poetry in the Human Relations Indie Book Prize for 2018. She has received seven Pushcart Prize nominations. Visit her website: triciaknoll.com

KATHERINE LEIGH was raised in a family of poets and wrote verse at an early age. Her influences were Robert Frost, Gerard Manley Hopkins, and Edna St. Vincent Millay. She served her seacoast community as Portsmouth Poet Laureate from 2015 to 2017, working with children on themes of social justice through the project Poems For Peace. "Don Hall taught me by his example never to give up on what I call 'inner prompts,' no matter what others might think or say about one's work."

JIM MELLO writes his poems on the run due to his day jobs as Counselor/Clinical Supervisor, Pastor, and Adjunct Professor at the University of Maine at Farmington. Donald Hall's decision to live at Eagle Pond and his interview in *Poets & Writers* role modeled for him to keep art and nature at the center of his life, and gave him encouragement that the muse keeps whispering to us throughout our lives. Jim finds solace and inspiration in music, nature, and the cosmos. Jim has two chapbooks, *Early Late Bloom*, and *All Four Seasons* (Moon Pie Press), and a self-published volume of poems, *For the Love of the Words*. Individual poems have been published in Bangor Theological Seminary's newsletter, and Goose River Press anthologies.

MARK MELNICOVE is the author of *Sometimes Times*, a portfolio of poems in response to prints by Terry Winters, published in a limited edition by Two Palms Press, NYC, in 2017. *Ghosts*, a series of his poems in dialogue with paintings of ghosts by Abby Shahn, was published in 2018. His poems have appeared in *Agni*, *The Café Review*, *Gargoyle*, and Maine Public Radio's *Poems from Here*. He is the co-author of *The Uncensored Guide to Maine*, and *Africa Is Not a Country*. He teaches English and creative writing at Falmouth High School, Falmouth, Maine. He has been inspired by Donald Hall's changes over time—not only in his approaches to poem writing, but also life living, death dying.

ANDREW PERIALE is a playwright, puppeteer, poet and polyglot. He is a member of City Hall Poets (Portsmouth, New Hampshire), and was for four years the poet laureate of Rochester, New Hampshire. He performs two poetry-based one-man shows: *Mano-a-Monolog*, and *Forman Brown, New Hampshire's Forgotten Poet* (based on a man who was a protégé of Robert Frost). Periale has taught creative writing workshops at two Maine high schools for the past thirteen years. "One of the many ways Donald Hall influenced me was by reading multiple drafts of one of my favorite poems of his. His commitment to craft is legendary."

DAWN POTTER directs the Frost Place Conference on Poetry and Teaching, held each summer at Robert Frost's home in Franconia, New Hampshire. She is the author of eight books of prose and poetry, most recently, *Chestnut Ridge*, forthcoming. "Donald Hall was a long-time friend of the poetry programs at the Frost Place, and in a 2015 letter to me he told me that his wife, Jane Kenyon, had first read her famous poem 'Melancholy' to an audience in Frost's barn. He said, 'She paused to weep a little, at one point.' Don closed the letter with the words, 'I love what you are doing!'—such a gift from one poet to another, these words of encouragement and cheer. He was one of the great rural elegists, a poet of sadness and love, a writer who deeply engaged with the past. In such ways he has influenced me immeasurably."

KYLE POTVIN'S chapbook, *Sound Travels on Water* (Finishing Line Press), won the 2014 Jean Pedrick Chapbook Award. She is a two-time finalist for the Howard Nemerov Sonnet Award. Her poems have appeared in *Bellevue Literary Review*, *Crab Creek Review*, *JAMA*, *Measure*, *The New York Times*, and others. She is an advisor to Frost Farm Poetry in Derry, New Hampshire, and helps produce the New Hampshire Poetry Festival. She lives with her husband and two sons in southern New Hampshire. "When I was diagnosed with cancer in 2006, Donald Hall and Jane Kenyon were constant companions. They remain within arms' reach."

JESSICA PURDY holds an MFA in Creative Writing from Emerson College. Recently her poems have appeared in *Bluestem Magazine*, *The Light Ekphrastic*, and *The Wild Word*. Her chapbook, *Learning the Names*, was published in 2015 by Finishing Line Press. Her books *STARLAND* and *Sleep in a Strange House* were both released by Nixes Mate Books consecutively, in 2017 and 2018. "Donald Hall's book of essays, *Seasons at Eagle Pond*, has always been an influence on my poems because of his descriptions of the seasons in the surrounding landscape of New Hampshire, the home I love."

GARY RAINFORD is the author of *Salty Liquor* and *Liner Notes*. He lives on Swan's Island, Maine, year-round with his wife and daughter. Gary is polishing a new collection, a novel in poetry form, about his mother's first year living with Alzheimer's disease. These poems square off with the bitter reality, "To grow old is to lose everything," the opening line in Donald Hall's poem, "Affirmation." "Often I turn to Donald Hall's essays on growing old for a good laugh or a bit of strength."

STEVEN RATINER'S photo of Donald Hall appears on the front cover of this anthology. His poetry has appeared in numerous journals in America and abroad including *Agni*, *Consequence*, *Hanging Loose*, *Parnassus*, *Poet Lore*, *Poetry Australia*, *QRLS* (Singapore), and *Salamander*. He's written about poetry for *The Christian Science Monitor* and their media stations, *The San Francisco Chronicle*, *Horizon*, and *Yankee Magazine*; for the past several years, he reviewed poetry for *The Washington Post*. *Giving Their Word*, a collection of interviews, was re-issued in a paperback edition from University of Massachusetts Press and includes conversations with some of poetry's most vital contemporary voices such as Seamus Heaney, Mary Oliver, Bei Dao, and the last full-length interview with Bill Stafford before he died. "I am proud to say that Donald Hall—the only poet interviewed twice in the collection—was a mentor and a friend."

DAVE CONLIN READ has resided in the Berkshires since the 1980s, working in education and public relations, including twenty years writing Tanglewood concert reviews for BerkshireLinks.com. "Between June 2012 and November 2017, I enjoyed an acquaintance with Donald Hall that included several letters and three visits to Eagle Pond Farm (and various restaurants), plus his last poetry reading and talk at UNH. Writing to congratulate him on the UNH event, I summarized our acquaintance as a 'tuition-free seminar for me,' and included my poem 'Afterparty.' In his response, dated Dec. 8, 2017, he wrote, 'I like Afterparty.'"

RUSSELL ROWLAND is a retired church pastor from New Hampshire's Lakes Region, whose work has appeared in many journals and received numerous awards, including seven Pushcart Prize nominations. Two chapbooks are available from Finishing Line Press, and a full-length collection, *We're All Home Now*, from Beech River Books. "After a poetry reading by Donald Hall in Bradford, New Hampshire in 1998, I had the temerity to hand him a sheaf of my own poems. Within a week I received a postcard of thanks and encouragement, a kindness I'll not soon forget."

CLEMENS SCHOENEBECK has had his work published in *the Aurorean, Caribbean Writer, Ibbetson Street, Miramar, Midwest Poetry Review*, and others. A four-time Pushcart Prize nominee, he is author of the memoir, *Dancing with Fireflies*. A collection of selected poems, *Where the Time Went: Poems at Eighty*, was recently published by Encircle Publications. Seeing Donald Hall and Jane Kenyon at a reading in Wilmot New Hampshire and in Bill Moyers' "A Life Together" inspired Schoenebeck. "I was so impressed that their presentation was conversational, understandable, so ordinary. I could understand them. Prior to that, I always assumed poetry was mysterious, very academic, and beyond me!"

JOHN SUROWIECKI is the author of six chapbooks and five full collections of poetry, the latest being *Martha Playing Wiffle Ball in Her Wedding Dress and Other Poems*, published by Encircle Publications. He has won a number of awards, including the Poetry Foundation Pegasus Award for verse drama, the *Nimrod* Pablo Neruda Prize and the silver medal in the Sunken Garden National Competition. Publications include: *Alaska Quarterly Review, Carolina Quarterly, Folio, Gargoyle, Margie, Mississippi Review, Oyez Review, Poetry, Prairie Schooner, Redivider, Rhino, The Southern Review, Tupelo Quarterly, West Branch, Yemassee*, and others. His first novel, *Pie Man*, won the Nilson Prize for a First Novel. "I grew up in Meriden, Connecicut, two towns from Hamden where Hall grew up. His 'The Sleeping Giant' was always a favorite of mine because in Meriden we looked at the same range of hills, although ours was in the shape of a train rather than a sleeping giant."

WALLY SWIST'S new books include *Singing for Nothing: Selected Nonfiction as Literary Memoir* (The Operating System), *The Map of Eternity* (Shanti Arts), and *On Beauty* (Adelaide Books). "Donald Hall influenced me in many ways, beginning with my reading his handsome volume published by David R. Godine, *The Town of Hill*, in 1975; his books *Kicking the Leaves* and *Remembering Poets* became favorites of mine, in 1978; and when I hosted Don at Trinity College in 1999, he read the poems he wrote after Jane Kenyon's death from *Without*. The reading stands as one of the most moving I've ever heard."

JERI THERIAULT'S *In the Museum of Surrender* won the 2013 Encircle Publications chapbook contest. In July 2016, Moon Pie Press released a full collection, *Radost, my red*. She has two other chapbooks and her work has appeared in such venues as: *The American Journal of Poetry, The Atlanta Review, The Beloit Poetry Journal, The Paterson Literary Review, Rhino*, and in *Deep Water* and *Poems from Here*. A three-time Pushcart Prize nominee and a Fulbright recipient, she holds an MFA from VCFA. She lives in South Portland, Maine. "I admire the way Donald Hall creates characters by his meticulous attention to ordinary detail; 'Ox-Cart Man' is a long-time favorite."

IRENE WILLIS has authored five poetry collections, most recently *Rehearsal* (IPBooks, 2018), and has edited an anthology, *Climate of Opinion: Sigmund Freud in Poetry* (IPBooks, 2017). A longtime educator, she is currently Poetry Editor of the online publication, *International Psychoanalysis*. She writes, "I have long been inspired by Donald Hall's everyday scenes and language, deep country wisdom and keen awareness of love, death and the passage of time."

WARREN WOESSNER is the co-founder and Senior Editor of *Abraxas*. His poetry has been widely published in reviews and journals, including *5 AM, Appalachia, Cutbank, Epoch, Iconoclast, Living Wilderness, The Nation, Osiris, Poetry*, and *Poetry Now*. He has received Fellowships from the NEA, The Wisconsin Arts Board, and the McKnight Foundation. Woessner works as a patent attorney and spends most of his time on Martha's Vineyard. "A.R. Ammons, my first poetry teacher, once told me that the last lines of a successful poem should 'push the poem over the edge.' Donald Hall's poetry does that for me. Many of his poems start out like simple conversations, but end with sudden turns of thought that take me into unexpected places."

JANE YOLEN is the author of 370 published books, including ten books of adult poetry, the first from Algonquin Books, Holy!Cow Press. Many of her poems have appeared in journals, magazines, and anthologies, including one that Billy Collins edited. She's lived in Massachusetts since 1966. Yolen is the first writer to be given the New England National Public Radio's Arts & Humanities award. She writes a poem a day for over 1,000 subscribers, and has received honorary doctorates from six New England colleges and universities for her body of work. Donald Hall and she taught together at Centrum Writer's Conference and enjoyed a correspondence over the years.

ANTHOLOGY EDITOR CYNTHIA BRACKETT-VINCENT has published/edited *the Aurorean* poetry journal continuously since 1995, giving voice to over 1,500 poets worldwide. She holds a BFA in creative writing from the University of Maine at Farmington. She serves as lead/acquisitions editor for Encircle Publications, which she co-owns with her husband Eddie Vincent. Encircle publishes full-length poetry and fiction books with an emphasis on mystery novels. Originally from Plymouth, Massachusetts where she co-founded the Tidepool Poets, she regularly visits her six grandchildren there. Her poetry, creative nonfiction, essays, and educational writing have been published in the United States and abroad in such venues as *frogpond*, *Ibbetson Street*, *Pirene's Fountain*, *The Cape Cod Poetry Review*, *The Penman Review*, and *Yankee Magazine*. Cynthia's co-edited *Women on Poetry: Writing, Revising, Publishing & Teaching* (McFarland) was named "One of 100 Best Books for Writers" by *Poets & Writers*. Her poetry has been nominated for the Pushcart Prize, and she has been the recipient of a Norton Island residency in poetry. She facilitates a yearly poetry workshop at Pyramid Life Center in the Adirondacks.

INTRODUCTORY TRIBUTE AUTHOR WESLEY MCNAIR, former Poet Laureate of Maine, has been called by poet Philip Levine "one of the great storytellers of contemporary poetry." He is the author of ten volumes of poems and twenty books, including poetry, nonfiction, and edited anthologies. McNair has held grants from the Fulbright and Guggenheim foundations, two Rockefeller grants for study at the Bellagio Center in Italy, two NEA fellowships, and a United States Artist Fellowship as one of America's "finest living artists." He has twice been invited to read his poetry by the Library of Congress, and has served five times on the Pulitzer jury for the Pulitzer Prize in poetry. Other honors include the Robert Frost Award, the Theodore Roethke Prize, an Emmy Award, and the Sarah Josepha Hale Medal, for his "distinguished contribution to the world of letters." His poetry has been featured on NPR's Weekend Edition and twenty-three times on Garrison Keillor's Writer's Almanac. It has also appeared in *Best American Poetry* and over sixty anthologies and textbooks. In 2015 he was named as the recipient of the 2015 PEN New England Award for Literary Excellence in Poetry. Colby College hosts his online "Letters Between Poets"—1976–1984 letters between him and Donald Hall. His new book is *The Unfastening*.